The Author's Farce by Her

Henry Fielding was born at Sharpham Park, near Glastonbury, in Somerset on April 22nd 1707. His early years were spent on his parents' farm in Dorset before being educated at Eton.

An early romance ended disastrously and with it his removal to London and the beginnings of a glittering literary career; he published his first play, at age 21, in 1728.

He was prolific, sometimes writing six plays a year, but he did like to poke fun at the authorities. His plays were thought to be the final straw for the authorities in their attempts to bring in a new law. In 1737 The Theatrical Licensing Act was passed. At a stroke political satire was almost impossible. Fielding was rendered mute. Any playwright who was viewed with suspicion by the Government now found an audience difficult to find and therefore Theatre owners now toed the Government line.

Fielding was practical with the circumstances and ironically stopped writing to once again take up his career in the practice of law and became a barrister after studying at Middle Temple. By this time he had married Charlotte Craddock, his first wife, and they would go on to have five children. Charlotte died in 1744 but was immortalised as the heroine in both Tom Jones and Amelia.

Fielding was put out by the success of Samuel Richardson's Pamela, or Virtue Rewarded. His reaction was to spur him into writing a novel. In 1741 his first novel was published; the successful Shamela, an anonymous parody of Richardson's novel.

Undoubtedly the masterpiece of Fielding's career was the novel Tom Jones, published in 1749. It is a wonderfully and carefully constructed picaresque novel following the convoluted and hilarious tale of how a foundling came into a fortune.

Fielding was a consistent anti-Jacobite and a keen supporter of the Church of England. This led to him now being richly rewarded with the position of London's Chief Magistrate. Fielding continued to write and his career both literary and professional continued to climb.

In 1749 he joined with his younger half-brother John, to help found what was the nascent forerunner to a London police force, the Bow Street Runners. Fielding's ardent commitment to the cause of justice in the 1750s unfortunately coincided with a rapid deterioration in his health. Such was his decline that in the summer of 1754 he travelled, with Mary and his daughter, to Portugal in search of a cure. Gout, asthma, dropsy and other afflictions forced him to use crutches. His health continued to fail alarmingly.

Henry Fielding died in Lisbon two months later on October 8th, 1754.

Index of Contents

THE AUTHOR'S FARCE; WITH A PUPPET-SHOW CALLED THE PLEASURES OF THE TOWN

FIRST ACTED AT THE HAY-MARKET IN 1729, AND REVIVED SOME YEARS AFTER AT DRURY-LANE, WHEN IT WAS REVISED AND GREATLY ALTERED BY THE AUTHOR, AS NOW PRINTED.

PERSONS IN THE FARCE
MEN

Luckless, the Author and Master of the Show	Mr Mullart
Witmore, his friend	Mr Lacy
Marplay, sen., Comedian	Mr Reynolds
Marplay, jun., Comedian	Mr Stopler
Bookweight, a Bookseller	Mr Jones
Scarecrow, Scribbler	Mr Marshal
Dash, Scribbler	Mr Hallam
Quibble, Scribbler	Mr Dove
Blotpage, Scribbler	Mr Wells, junior
Index	
Jack, servant to Luckless	Mr Achurch
Jack-Pudding	Mr Reynolds

Bantomite	Mr Marshal
WOMEN	
Mrs Moneywood, the Author's Landlady	Mrs Mullart
Harriot, her daughter	Miss Palms

PROLOGUE, SPOKEN BY MR JONES

Too long the Tragick Muse hath aw'd the stage,
And frighten'd wives and children with her rage,
Too long Drawcansir roars, Parthenope weeps,
While ev'ry lady cries, and critick sleeps
With ghosts, rapes, murders, tender hearts they wound,
Or else, like thunder, terrify with sound
When the skill'd actress to her weeping eyes,
With artful sigh, the handkerchief applies,
How griev'd each sympathizing nymph appears!
And box and gallery both melt in tears
Or when, in armour of Corinthian brass,
Heroick actor stares you in the face,
And cries aloud, with emphasis that's fit, on
Liberty, freedom, liberty and Briton!
While frowning, gaping for applause he stands,
What generous Briton can refuse his hands?
Like the tame animals design'd for show,
You have your cues to clap, as they to bow,
Taught to commend, your judgments have no share,
By chance you guess aright, by chance you err.
But, handkerchiefs and Britain laid aside,
To-night we mean to laugh, and not to chide.
In days of yore, when fools were held in fashion,
Tho' now, alas! all banish'd from the nation,
A merry jester had reform'd his lord,
Who would have scorn'd the sterner Stoick's word
Bred in Democritus his laughing schools,
Our author flies sad Heraclitus rules,
No tears, no terror plead in his behalf,
The aim of Farce is but to make you laugh
Beneath the tragick or the comick name,
Farces and puppet shows ne'er miss of fame
Since then, in borrow'd dress, they've pleas'd the town,
Condemn them not, appearing in their own
Smiles we expect from the good-natur'd few,
As ye are done by, ye malicious, do,
And kindly laugh at him who laughs at you.

ACT I

SCENE I.—Luckless's Room in Mrs Moneywood's House

MRS MONEYWOOD, HARRIOT, LUCKLESS.

MRS MONEYWOOD
Never tell me, Mr Luckless, of your play, and your play. I tell you I must be paid. I would no more depend on a benefit-night of an unacted play than I would on a benefit-ticket in an undrawn lottery. Could I have guessed that I had a poet in my house! Could I have looked for a poet under laced clothes!

LUCKLESS
Why not? since you may often find poverty under them: nay, they are commonly the signs of it. And, therefore, why may not a poet be seen in them as well as a courtier?

MRS MONEYWOOD
Do you make a jest of my misfortune, sir?

LUCKLESS
Rather my misfortune. I am sure I have a better title to poverty than you; for, notwithstanding the handsome figure I make, unless you are so good to invite me, I am afraid I shall scarce prevail on my stomach to dine to-day.

MRS MONEYWOOD
Oh, never fear that—you will never want a dinner till you have dined at all the eating-houses round.— No one shuts their doors against you the first time; and I think you are so kind, seldom to trouble them a second.

LUCKLESS
No.—And if you will give me leave to walk out of your doors, the devil take me if ever I come into 'em again,

MRS MONEYWOOD
Pay me, sir, what you owe me, and walk away whenever you please.

LUCKLESS
With all my heart, madam; get me a pen and ink, and I'll give you my note for it immediately.

MRS MONEYWOOD
Your note! who will discount it? Not your bookseller; for he has as many of your notes as he has of your works; both good lasting ware, and which are never likely to go out of his shop and his scrutore.

HARRIOT
Nay, but, madam, 'tis barbarous to insult him in this manner.

MRS MONEYWOOD

No doubt you'll take his part. Pray get you about your business. I suppose he intends to pay me by ruining you. Get you in this instant: and remember, if ever I see you with him again I'll turn you out of doors.

SCENE II

LUCKLESS, MRS MONEYWOOD

LUCKLESS
Discharge all your ill-nature on me, madam, but spare poor Miss Harriot.

MRS MONEYWOOD
Oh! then it is plain. I have suspected your familiarity a long while. You are a base man. Is it not enough to stay three months in my house without paying me a farthing, but you must ruin my child?

LUCKLESS
I love her as my soul. Had I the world I'd give it her all.

MRS MONEYWOOD
But, as you happen to have nothing in the world, I desire you would have nothing to say to her. I suppose you would have settled all your castles in the air. Oh! I wish you had lived in one of them, instead of my house. Well, I am resolved, when you have gone away (which I heartily hope will be very soon) I'll hang over my door in great red letters, "No lodgings for poets." Sure never was such a guest as you have been. My floor is all spoiled with ink, my windows with verses, and my door has been almost beat down with duns.

LUCKLESS
Would your house had been beaten down, and everything but my dear Harriot crushed under it!

MRS MONEYWOOD
Sir, sir—

LUCKLESS
Madam, madam! I will attack you at your own weapons; I will pay you in your own coin.

MRS MONEYWOOD
I wish you'd pay me in any coin, sir.

LUCKLESS
Look ye, madam, I'll do as much as a reasonable woman can require; I'll shew you all I have; and give you all I have too, if you please to accept it.

[Turns his pockets Inside out.

MRS MONEYWOOD
I will not be used in this manner. No, sir, I will be paid, if there be any such thing as law.

LUCKLESS

By what law you will put money into my pocket I know not; for I never heard of any one who got money by the law but the lawyers. I have told you already, and I tell you again, that the first money I get shall be yours; and I have great expectations from my play. In the mean time your staying here can be of no service, and you may possibly drive some line thoughts out of my head. I would write a love scene, and your daughter would be more proper company, on that occasion, than you.

MRS MONEYWOOD

You would act a love-scene, I believe; but I shall prevent you; for I intend to dispose of myself before my daughter.

LUCKLESS

Dispose of yourself!

MRS MONEYWOOD

Yes, sir, dispose of myself. 'Tis very well known that I have had very good offers since my last dear husband died. I might have had an attorney of New Inn, or Mr Fillpot, the exciseman; yes, I had my choice of two parsons, or a doctor of physick; and yet I slighted them all; yes, I slighted them for—for—for you.

LUCKLESS

For me?

MRS MONEYWOOD [Sobbing]

Yes, you have seen too visible marks of my passion; too visible for my reputation.

LUCKLESS

I have heard very loud tokens of your passion; but I rather took it for the passion of anger than of love.

MRS MONEYWOOD

Oh! it was love, indeed. Nothing but love, upon my soul!

LUCKLESS

The devil! This way of dunning is worse than the other.

MRS MONEYWOOD

If thou can'st not pay me in money, let me have it in love. If I break through the modesty of my sex let my passion excuse it. I know the world will call it an impudent action; but if you will let me reserve all I have to myself, I will make myself yours for ever.

LUCKLESS

Toll, loll, loll!

MRS MONEYWOOD

And is this the manner you receive my declaration, you poor beggarly fellow? You shall repent this; remember, you shall repent it; remember that. I'll shew you the revenge of an injured woman.

LUCKLESS
I shall never repent anything that rids me of you, I am sure.

SCENE III

LUCKLESS, HARRIOT.

LUCKLESS
Dear Harriot!

HARRIOT
I have waited an opportunity to return to you.

LUCKLESS
Oh! my dear, I am so sick!

HARRIOT
What's the matter?

LUCKLESS
Oh! your mother! your mother!

HARRIOT
What, has she been scolding ever since?

LUCKLESS
Worse, worse!

HARRIOT
Heaven forbid she should threaten to go to law with you.

LUCKLESS
Oh, worse! worse! she threatens to go to church with me. She has made me a generous offer, that if I will but marry her she will suffer me to settle all she has upon her.

HARRIOT
Generous creature! Sure you will not resist the proposal?

LUCKLESS
Hum! what would you advise me to?

HARRIOT
Oh, take her, take her, by all means; you will be the prettiest, finest, loveliest, sweetest couple. Augh! what a delicate dish of matrimony you will make! Her age with your youth, her avarice with your extravagance, and her scolding with your poetry.

LUCKLESS
Nay, but I am serious, and I desire you would be so. You know my unhappy circumstances, and your mother's wealth. It would be at least a prudent match.

HARRIOT
Oh! extremely prudent, ha, ha, ha! the world will say, Lard! who could have thought Mr Luckless had had so much prudence? This one action will overbalance all the follies of your life.

LUCKLESS
Faith, I think it will: but, dear Harriot, how can I think of losing you for ever? And yet, as our affairs stand, I see no possibility of our being happy together. It will be some pleasure, too, that I may have it in my power to serve you. Believe me, it is with the utmost reluctance I think of parting with you. For if it was in my power to have you—

HARRIOT
Oh, I am very much obliged to you; I believe you—Yes, you need not swear, I believe you.

LUCKLESS
And can you as easily consult prudence, and part with me? for I would not buy my own happiness at the price of yours.

HARRIOT
I thank you, sir—Part with you—intolerable vanity!

LUCKLESS
Then I am resolved; and so, my good landlady, have at you.

HARRIOT [Crying]
Stay, sir, let me acquaint you with one thing—you are a villain! and don't think I'm vexed at anything, but that I should have been such a fool as ever to have had a good opinion of you.

LUCKLESS
Ha, ha, ha! Caught, by Jupiter! And did my dear Harriot think me in earnest?

HARRIOT
And was you not in earnest?

LUCKLESS
What, to part with thee? A pretty woman will be sooner in earnest to part with her beauty, or a great man with his power.

HARRIOT
I wish I were assured of the sincerity of your love.

AIR: Butter'd Pease.

LUCKLESS
Does my dearest Harriot ask

What for love I would pursue?
Would you, charmer, know what task
I would undertake for you?
Ask the bold ambitious, what
He for honours would atchieve?
Or the gay voluptuous, that
Which he'd not for pleasure give?
Ask the miser what he'd do
To amass excessive gain?
Or the saint, what he'd pursue,
His wish'd heav'n to obtain?
These I would attempt, and more—
For, oh! my Harriot is to me
All ambition, pleasure, store,
Or what heav'n itself can be!

HARRIOT
Would my dearest Luckless know
What his constant Harriot can
Her tender love and faith to show
For her dear, her only man?
Ask the vain coquette what she
For men's adoration would;
Or from censure to be free,
Ask the vile censorious prude.
In a coach and six to ride,
What the mercenary jade,
Or the widow to be bride
To a brisk broad-shoulder'd blade.
All these I would attempt for thee,
Could I but thy passion fix;
Thy will my sole commander be,
And thy arms my coach and six.

MRS MONEYWOOD [Within]
Harriot, Harriot.

HARRIOT
Hear the dreadful summons! adieu. I will take the first opportunity of seeing you again.

LUCKLESS
Adieu, my pretty charmer; go thy ways for the first of thy sex.

SCENE IV

LUCKLESS, JACK.

LUCKLESS
So! what news bring you?

JACK
An't please your honour I have been at my lord's, and his lordship thanks you for the favour you have offered of reading your play to him; but he has such a prodigious deal of business, he begs to be excused. I have been with Mr Keyber too—he made me no answer at all. Mr Bookweight will be here immediately.

LUCKLESS

JACK

JACK
Sir.

LUCKLESS
Fetch my other hat hither;—carry it to the pawnbroker's.

JACK
To your honour's own pawnbroker!

LUCKLESS
Ay—and in thy way home call at the cook's shop. So, one way or other, I find my head must always provide for my belly.

SCENE V

LUCKLESS, **WITMORE**.

LUCKLESS
I am surprized! dear Witmore!

WITMORE
Dear Harry!

LUCKLESS
This is kind, indeed; but I do not more wonder at finding a man in this age who can be a friend to adversity, than that Fortune should be so much my friend as to direct you to me; for she is a lady I have not been much indebted to lately.

WITMORE
She who told me, I assure you, is one you have been indebted to a long while.

LUCKLESS
Whom do you mean?

WITMORE
One who complains of your unkindness in not visiting her—Mrs Lovewood.

LUCKLESS
Dost thou visit there still, then?

WITMORE
I throw an idle hour away there sometimes. When I am in an ill-humour I am sure of feeding it there with all the scandal in town, for no bawd is half so diligent in looking after girls with an uncracked maidenhead as she in searching out women with cracked reputations.

LUCKLESS
The much more infamous office of the two.

WITMORE
Thou art still a favourer of the women, I find.

LUCKLESS
Ay, the women and the muses—the high roads to beggary.

WITMORE
What, art thou not cured of scribling yet?

LUCKLESS
No, scribling is as impossible to cure as the gout.

WITMORE
And as sure a sign of poverty as the gout of riches. 'Sdeath! in an age of learning and true politeness, where a man might succeed by his merit, there would be some encouragement. But now, when party and prejudice carry all before them; when learning is decried, wit not understood; when the theatres are puppet-shows, and the comedians ballad-singers; when fools lead the town, would a man think to thrive by his wit? If you must write, write nonsense, write operas, write Hurlothrumbos, set up an oratory and preach nonsense, and you may meet with encouragement enough. Be profane, be scurrilous, be immodest: if you would receive applause, deserve to receive sentence at the Old Bailey; and if you would ride in a coach, deserve to ride in a cart.

LUCKLESS
You are warm, my friend.

WITMORE
It is because I am your friend. I cannot bear to hear the man I love ridiculed by fools—by idiots. To hear a fellow who, had he been born a Chinese, had starved for want of genius to have been even the lowest mechanick, toss up his empty noddle with an affected disdain of what he has not understood; and women abusing what they have neither seen nor heard, from an unreasonable prejudice to an honest fellow whom they have not known. If thou wilt write against all these reasons get a patron, be pimp to

some worthless man of quality, write panegyricks on him, flatter him with as many virtues as he has vices. Then, perhaps, you will engage his lordship, his lordship engages the town on your side, and then write till your arms ake, sense or nonsense, it will all go down.

LUCKLESS
Thou art too satirical on mankind. It is possible to thrive in the world by justifiable means.

WITMORE
Ay, justifiable, and so they are justifiable by custom. What does the soldier or physician thrive by but slaughter?—the lawyer but by quarrels?—the courtier but by taxes?—the poet but by flattery? I know none that thrive by profiting mankind, but the husbandman and the merchant: the one gives you the fruit of your own soil, the other brings you those from abroad; and yet these are represented as mean and mechanical, and the others as honourable and glorious.

LUCKLESS
Well; but prithee leave railing, and tell me what you would advise me to do.

WITMORE
Do! why thou art a vigorous young fellow, and there are rich widows in town.

LUCKLESS
But I am already engaged.

WITMORE
Why don't you marry then—for I suppose you are not mad enough to have any engagement with a poor mistress?

LUCKLESS
Even so, faith; and so heartily that I would not change her for the widow of a Croesus.

WITMORE
Now thou art undone, indeed. Matrimony clenches ruin beyond retrieval. What unfortunate stars wert thou born under? Was it not enough to follow those nine ragged jades the muses, but you must fasten on some earth-born mistress as poor as them?

MARPLAY JNR [Within]
Order my chairman to call on me at St James's.—No, let them stay.

WITMORE
Heyday, whom the devil have we here?

LUCKLESS
The young captain, sir; no less a person, I assure you.

SCENE VI

LUCKLESS, WITMORE, MARPLAY JNR.

MARPLAY JNR
Mr Luckless, I kiss your hands—Sir, I am your most obedient humble servant; you see, Mr Luckless, what power you have over me. I attend your commands, though several persons of quality have staid at court for me above this hour.

LUCKLESS
I am obliged to you—I have a tragedy for your house, Mr Marplay.

MARPLAY JNR
Ha! if you will send it to me, I will give you my opinion of it; and if I can make any alterations in it that will be for its advantage, I will do it freely.

WITMORE
Alterations, sir?

MARPLAY JNR
Yes, sir, alterations—I will maintain it. Let a play be never so good, without alteration it will do nothing.

WITMORE
Very odd indeed!

MARPLAY JNR
Did you ever write, sir?

WITMORE
No, sir, I thank Heaven.

MARPLAY JNR
Oh! your humble servant—your very humble servant, sir. When you write yourself, you will find the necessity of alterations. Why, sir, would you guess that I had altered Shakspeare?

WITMORE
Yes, faith, sir, no one sooner.

MARPLAY JNR
Alack-a-day! Was you to see the plays when they are brought to us—a parcel of crude undigested stuff. We are the persons, sir, who lick them into form—that mould them into shape. The poet make the play indeed! the colourman might be as well said to make the picture, or the weaver the coat. My father and I, sir, are a couple of poetical tailors. When a play is brought us, we consider it as a tailor does his coat: we cut it, sir—we cut it; and let me tell you we have the exact measure of the town; we know how to fit their taste. The poets, between you and me, are a pack of ignorant——

WITMORE
Hold, hold, sir. This is not quite so civil to Mr Luckless; besides, as I take it, you have done the town the honour of writing yourself.

MARPLAY JNR

Sir, you are a man of sense, and express yourself well. I did, as you say, once make a small sally into Parnassus—took a sort of flying leap over Helicon; but if ever they catch me there again—sir, the town have a prejudice to my family; for, if any play could have made them ashamed to damn it, mine must. It was all over plot. It would have made half a dozen novels: nor was it crammed with a pack of wit-traps, like Congreve and Wycherly, where every one knows when the joke was coming. I defy the sharpest critick of them all to have known when any jokes of mine were coming. The dialogue was plain, easy, and natural, and not one single joke in it from the beginning to the end: besides, sir, there was one scene of tender melancholy conversation—enough to have melted a heart of stone; and yet they damned it—and they damned themselves; for they shall have no more of mine.

WITMORE

Take pity on the town, sir.

MARPLAY JNR

I! No, sir, no. I'll write no more. No more; unless I am forced to it.

LUCKLESS

That's no easy thing, Marplay.

MARPLAY JNR

Yes, sir. Odes, odes, a man may be obliged to write those, you know.

LUCKLESS and **WITMORE**

Ha, ha, ha! that's true indeed.

LUCKLESS

But about my tragedy, Mr Marplay.

MARPLAY JNR

I believe my father is at the playhouse: if you please, we will read it now; but I must call on a young lady first—Hey, who's there? Is my footman there? Order my chair to the door. Your servant, gentlemen.— Caro vien.

[Exit, singing.

WITMORE

This is the most finished gentleman I ever saw; and hath not, I dare swear, his equal.

LUCKLESS

If he has, here he comes.

SCENE VII

LUCKLESS, WITMORE, BOOKWEIGHT.

LUCKLESS

Mr Bookweight, your very humble servant.

BOOKWEIGHT

I was told, sir, that you had particular business with me.

LUCKLESS

Yes, Mr Bookweight; I have something to put into your hands. I have a play for you, Mr Bookweight.

BOOKWEIGHT

Is it accepted, sir?

LUCKLESS

Not yet.

BOOKWEIGHT

Oh, sir! when it is, it will be then time enough to talk about it. A play, like a bill, is of no value till it is accepted; nor indeed when it is, very often. Besides, sir, our playhouses are grown so plenty, and our actors so scarce, that really plays are become very bad commodities. But pray, sir, do you offer it to the players or the patentees?

LUCKLESS

Oh! to the players, certainly.

BOOKWEIGHT

You are in the right of that. But a play which will do on the stage will not always do for us; there are your acting plays and your reading plays.

WITMORE

I do not understand that distinction.

BOOKWEIGHT

Why, sir, your acting play is entirely supported by the merit of the actor; in which case, it signifies very little whether there be any sense in it or no. Now, your reading play is of a different stamp, and must have wit and meaning in it. These latter I call your substantive, as being able to support themselves. The former are your adjective, as what require the buffoonery and gestures of an actor to be joined with them to shew their signification.

WITMORE

Very learnedly defined, truly.

LUCKLESS

Well, but, Mr Bookweight, will you advance fifty guineas on my play?

BOOKWEIGHT

Fifty guineas! Yes, sir. You shall have them with all my heart, if you will give me security for them. Fifty guineas for a play! Sir, I would not give fifty shillings.

LUCKLESS

'Sdeath, sir! do you beat me down at this rate?

BOOKWEIGHT

No, nor fifty farthings. Fifty guineas! Indeed your name is well worth that.

LUCKLESS

Jack, take this worthy gentleman and kick him down stairs.

BOOKWEIGHT

Sir, I shall make you repent this.

JACK

Come, sir, will you please to brush?

BOOKWEIGHT

Help! murder! I'll have the law of you, sir.

LUCKLESS

Ha, ha, ha!

SCENE VIII

LUCKLESS, WITMORE, MRS MONEYWOOD.

MRS MONEYWOOD

What noise is this? It is a very fine thing, truly, Mr Luckless, that you will make these uproars in my house.

LUCKLESS

If you dislike it, it is in your power to drown a much greater. Do you but speak, madam, and I am sure no one will be heard but yourself.

MRS MONEYWOOD

Very well, indeed! fine reflexions on my character! Sir, sir, all the neighbours know that I have been as quiet a woman as ever lived in the parish. I had no noises in my house till you came. We were the family of love. But you have been a nusance to the whole neighbourhood. While you had money, my doors were thundered at every morning at four and five, by coachmen and chairmen; and since you have had none, my house has been besieged all day by creditors and bailiffs. Then there's the rascal your man; but I will pay the dog, I will scour him. Sir, I am glad you are a witness of his abuses of me.

WITMORE

I am indeed, madam, a witness how unjustly he has abused you.

[**JACK** whispers **LUCKLESS**.

LUCKLESS

Witmore, excuse me a moment.

MRS MONEYWOOD, WITMORE.

MRS MONEYWOOD

Yes, sir; and, sir, a man that has never shewn one the colour of his money.

WITMORE

Very hard, truly. How much may he be in your debt, pray? Because he has ordered me to pay you.

MRS MONEYWOOD

Ay! sir, I wish he had.

WITMORE

I am serious, I assure you.

MRS MONEYWOOD

I am very glad to hear it, sir. Here is the bill as we settled it this very morning. I always thought, indeed, Mr Luckless had a great deal of honesty in his principles: any man may be unfortunate; but I knew when he had money I should have it; and what signifies dunning a man when he hath it not? Now that is a way with some people which I could never come in to.

WITMORE

There, madam, is your money. You may give Mr Luckless the receipt.

MRS MONEYWOOD

Sir, I give you both a great many thanks. I am sure it is almost as charitable as if you gave it me; for I am to make up a sum to-morrow morning. Well, if Mr Luckless was but a little soberer I should like him for a lodger exceedingly: for I must say, I think him a very pleasant good-humoured man.

SCENE X

LUCKLESS, WITMORE, MRS MONEYWOOD.

LUCKLESS

Those are words I never heard out of that mouth before.

MRS MONEYWOOD

Ha, ha, ha! you are pleased to be merry: ha, ha!

LUCKLESS

Why, Witmore, thou hast the faculty opposite to that of a witch, and canst lay a tempest. I should as soon have imagined one man could have stopt a cannon-ball in its full force as her tongue.

MRS MONEYWOOD
Ha, ha, ha! he is the best company in the world, sir, and so full of his similitudes!

WITMORE
Luckless, good morrow; I shall see you soon again.

LUCKLESS
Let it be soon, I beseech you; for thou hast brought a calm into this house that was scarce ever in it before.

SCENE XI

LUCKLESS, MRS MONEYWOOD, JACK.

MRS MONEYWOOD
Well, Mr Luckless, you are a comical man, to give one such a character to a stranger.

LUCKLESS
The company is gone, madam; and now, like true man and wife, we may fall to abusing one another as fast as we please.

MRS MONEYWOOD
Abuse me as you please, so you pay me, sir.

LUCKLESS
'Sdeath! madam, I will pay you.

MRS MONEYWOOD
Nay, sir, I do not ask it before it is due. I don't question your payment at all: if you was to stay in my house this quarter of a year, as I hope you will, I should not ask you for a farthing.

LUCKLESS
Toll, loll, loll.—But I shall have her begin with her passion immediately; and I had rather be the object of her rage for a year than of her love for half an hour.

MRS MONEYWOOD
But why did you choose to surprise me with my money? Why did you not tell me you would pay me?

LUCKLESS
Why, have I not told you?

MRS MONEYWOOD

Yes, you told me of a play, and stuff: but you never told me you would order a gentleman to pay me. A sweet, pretty, good-humoured gentleman he is, heaven bless him! Well, you have comical ways with you: but you have honesty at the bottom, and I'm sure the gentleman himself will own I gave you that character.

LUCKLESS
Oh! I smell you now.—You see, madam, I am better than my word to you: did he pay it you in gold or silver?

MRS MONEYWOOD
All pure gold.

LUCKLESS
I have a vast deal of silver, which he brought me, within; will you do me the favour of taking it in silver? that will be of use to you in the shop too.

MRS MONEYWOOD
Anything to oblige you, sir.

LUCKLESS
Jack, bring out the great bag, number one. Please to tell the money, madam, on that table.

MRS MONEYWOOD
It's easily told: heaven knows there's not so much on't.

JACK
Sir, the bag is so heavy, I cannot bring it in.

LUCKLESS
Why, then, come and help to thrust a heavier bag out.

MRS MONEYWOOD
What do you mean?

LUCKLESS
Only to pay you in my bed-chamber.

MRS MONEYWOOD
Villain, dog, I'll swear a robbery, and have you hanged: rogues, villains!

LUCKLESS
Be as noisy as you please—

[Shuts the door.

Jack, call a coach; and, d' ye hear? get up behind it and attend me.

ACT II

SCENE I.—The Playhouse

LUCKLESS, MARPLAY SENIOR, MARPLAY JUNIOR.

LUCKLESS
[Reads]
"Then hence my sorrow, hence my ev'ry fear;
No matter where, so we are bless'd together.
With thee, the barren rocks, where not one step
Of human race lies printed in the snow,
Look lovely as the smiling infant spring."

MARPLAY SNR
Augh! will you please to read that again, sir?

LUCKLESS
"Then hence my sorrow, hence my ev'ry fear."

MARPLAY SNR
"Then hence my sorrow."—Horror is a much better word.—And then in the second line—"No matter where, so we are bless'd together."—Undoubtedly, it should be, "No matter where, so somewhere we're together." Where is the question, somewhere is the answer.—Read on, sir.

LUCKLESS
"With thee,—"

MARPLAY SNR
No, no, I could alter those lines to a much better idea.
"With thee, the barren blocks, where not a bit
Of human face is painted on the bark,
Look green as Covent-garden in the spring."

LUCKLESS
Green as Covent-garden!

MARPLAY JNR
Yes, yes; Covent-garden market, where they sell greens.

LUCKLESS
Monstrous!

MARPLAY SNR
Pray, sir, read on.

LUCKLESS

"LEANDRA: oh, my Harmonio, I could hear thee still;
The nightingale to thee sings out of tune,
While on thy faithful breast my head reclines,
The downy pillow's hard; while from thy lips
I drink delicious draughts of nectar down,
Falernian wines seem bitter to my taste."

MARPLAY JNR
Here's meat, drink, singing, and lodging, egad.

LUCKLESS
He answers.

MARPLAY JNR
But, sir—

LUCKLESS
"Oh, let me pull thee, press thee to my heart,
Thou rising spring of everlasting sweets!
Take notice, Fortune, I forgive thee all!
Thou'st made Leandra mine. Thou flood of joy
Mix with my soul, and rush thro' ev'ry vein."

MARPLAY SNR
Those two last lines again if you please.

LUCKLESS
"Thou'st made," &c.

MARPLAY JNR
"—Thou flood of joy,
Mix with my soul and rush thro' ev'ry vein."
Those are two excellent lines indeed:
I never writ better myself: but, Sar——

LUCKLESS
"Leandra's mine, go bid the tongue of fate
Pronounce another word of bliss like that;
Search thro' the eastern mines and golden shores,
Where lavish Nature pours forth all her stores;
For to my lot could all her treasures fall,
I would not change Leandra for them all."
There ends act the first, and such an act as,
I believe, never was on this stage yet.

MARPLAY JNR
Nor never will, I hope.

MARPLAY SNR
Pray, sir, let me look at one thing. "Falernian wines seem bitter to my taste."
Pray, sir, what sort of wines may your Falernian be? for I never heard of them before; and I am sure, as I keep the best company, if there had been such sorts of wines, I should have tasted them. Tokay I have drank, and Lacrimas I have drank, but what your Falernian is, the devil take me if I can tell.

MARPLAY JNR
I fancy, father, these wines grow at the top of Parnassus.

LUCKLESS
Do they so, Mr Pert? why then I fancy you have never tasted them.

MARPLAY SNR
Suppose you should say the wines of Cape are bitter to my taste.

LUCKLESS
Sir, I cannot alter it.

MARPLAY SNR
Nor we cannot act it. It won't do, sir, and so you need give yourself no farther trouble about it.

LUCKLESS
What particular fault do you find?

MARPLAY JNR
Sar, there's nothing that touches me, nothing that is coercive to my passions.

LUCKLESS
Fare you well, sir: may another play be coercive to your passions.

SCENE II

MARPLAY SNR, MARPLAY JNR.

MARPLAY SNR
Ha, ha, ha!

MARPLAY JNR
What do you think of the play?

MARPLAY SNR
It may be a very good one, for aught I know: but I am resolved, since the town will not receive any of mine, they shall have none from any other. I'll keep them to their old diet.

MARPLAY JNR
But suppose they won't feed on't?

MARPLAY SNR
Then it shall be crammed down their throats.

MARPLAY JNR
I wish, father, you would leave me that art for a legacy, since I am afraid I am like to have no other from you.

MARPLAY SNR
'Tis buff, child, 'tis buff—true Corinthian brass; and, heaven be praised, tho' I have given thee no gold, I have given thee enough of that, which is the better inheritance of the two. Gold thou might'st have spent, but this is a lasting estate that will stick by thee all thy life.

MARPLAY JNR
What shall be done with that farce which was damned last night?

MARPLAY SNR
Give it them again to-morrow. I have told some persons of quality that it is a good thing, and I am resolved not to be in the wrong: let us see which will be weary first, the town of damning, or we of being damned.

MARPLAY JNR
Rat the town, I say.

MARPLAY SNR
That's a good boy; and so say I: but, prithee, what didst thou do with the comedy which I gave thee t'other day, that I thought a good one?

MARPLAY JNR
Did as you ordered me; returned it to the author, and told him it would not do.

MARPLAY SNR
You did well. If thou writest thyself, and that I know thou art very well qualified to do, it is thy interest to keep back all other authors of any merit, and be as forward to advance those of none.

MARPLAY JNR
But I am a little afraid of writing; for my writings, you know, have fared but ill hitherto.

MARPLAY SNR
That is because thou hast a little mistaken the method of writing. The art of writing, boy, is the art of stealing old plays, by changing the name of the play, and new ones, by changing the name of the author.

MARPLAY JNR
If it was not for these cursed hisses and catcalls—

MARPLAY SNR
Harmless musick, child, very harmless musick, and what, when one is but well seasoned to it, has no effect at all: for my part, I have been used to them.

MARPLAY JNR

Ay, and I have been used to them too, for that matter.

MARPLAY SNR

And stood them bravely too. Idle young actors are fond of applause, but, take my word for it, a clap is a mighty silly, empty thing, and does no more good than a hiss; and, therefore, if any man loves hissing, he may have his three shillings worth at me whenever he pleases.

[Exeunt.

SCENE III.—A Room in Bookweight's House

DASH, **BLOTPAGE**, **QUIBBLE**, writing at several tables.

DASH

Pox on't, I'm as dull as an ox, tho' I have not a bit of one within me. I have not dined these two days, and yet my head is as heavy as any alderman's or lord's. I carry about me symbols of all the elements; my head is as heavy as water, my pockets are as light as air, my appetite is as hot as fire, and my coat is as dirty as earth.

BLOTPAGE

Lend me your Bysshe, Mr Dash, I want a rhime for wind.

DASH

Why there's blind, and kind, and behind, and find, and mind: it is of the easiest termination imaginable; I have had it four times in a page.

BLOTPAGE

None of those words will do.

DASH

Why then you may use any that end in ond, or and, or end. I am never so exact: if the two last letters are alike, it will do very well. Read the verse.

BLOTPAGE

"Inconstant as the seas or as the wind."

DASH

What would you express in the next line?

BLOTPAGE

Nay, that I don't know, for the sense is out already. I would say something about inconstancy.

DASH

I can lend you a verse, and it will do very well too.

"Inconstancy will never have an end."
End rhymes very well with wind.

BLOTPAGE

It will do well enough for the middle of a poem.

DASH

Ay, ay, anything will do well enough for the middle of a poem. If you can but get twenty good lines to place at the beginning for a taste, it will sell very well.

QUIBBLE

So that, according to you, Mr Dash, a poet acts pretty much on the same principles with an oister-woman.

DASH

Pox take your simile, it has set my chaps a watering: but come, let us leave off work for a while, and hear Mr Quibble's song.

QUIBBLE

My pipes are pure and clear, and my stomach is as hollow as any trumpet in Europe.

DASH

Come, the song.

SONG.
AIR.
Ye Commons and Peers.
How unhappy's the fate
To live by one's pate,
And be forced to write hackney for bread!
An author's a joke
To all manner of folk,
Wherever he pops up his head, his head,
Wherever he pops up his head.
Tho' he mount on that hack,
Old Pegasus' back, And of Helicon drink till he burst,
Yet a curse of those streams,
Poetical dreams, They never can quench one's thirst, &c.
Ah! how should he fly
On fancy so high,
When his limbs are in durance and hold?
Or how should he charm,
With genius so warm,
When his poor naked body's a cold, &c.

SCENE IV

BOOKWEIGHT, DASH, QUIBBLE, BLOTPAGE.

BOOKWEIGHT
Fie upon it, gentlemen! what, not at your pens? Do you consider, Mr Quibble, that it is a fortnight since your Letter to a Friend in the Country was published? Is it not high time for an Answer to come out? At this rate, before your Answer is printed, your Letter will be forgot. I love to keep a controversy up warm. I have had authors who have writ a pamphlet in the morning, answered it in the afternoon, and answered that again at night.

QUIBBLE
Sir, I will be as expeditious as possible: but it is harder to write on this side the question, because it is the wrong side.

BOOKWEIGHT
Not a jot. So far on the contrary, that I have known some authors choose it as the properest to shew their genius. But let me see what you have produced; "With all deference to what that very learned and most ingenious person, in his Letter to a Friend in the Country, hath advanced." Very well, sir; for, besides that, it may sell more of the Letter: all controversial writers should begin with complimenting their adversaries, as prize-fighters kiss before they engage. Let it be finished with all speed. Well, Mr Dash, have you done that murder yet?

DASH
Yes, sir, the murder is done; I am only about a few moral reflexions to place before it.

BOOKWEIGHT
Very well: then Jet me have the ghost finished by this day se'nnight.

DASH
What sort of a ghost would you have this, sir? the last was a pale one.

BOOKWEIGHT
Then let this be a bloody one. Mr Quibble, you may lay by that life which you are about; for I hear the person is recovered, and write me out proposals for delivering five sheets of Mr Bailey's English Dictionary every week, till the whole be finished. If you do not know the form, you may copy the proposals for printing Bayle's Dictionary in the same manner. The same words will do for both.

[Enter **INDEX**.

So, Mr Index, what news with you?

INDEX
I have brought my bill, sir.

BOOKWEIGHT
What's here? For fitting the motto of Risum teneatis Amici to a dozen pamphlets, at sixpence per each, six shillings; for Omnia vincit Amor, et nos cedamus Amori, sixpence; for Difficile est Satyram non scribere, sixpence. Hum! hum! hum!—sum total for thirty-six Latin mottoes, eighteen shillings; ditto

English, one shilling and ninepence; ditto Greek, four—four shillings. These Greek mottoes are excessively dear.

INDEX
If you have them cheaper at either of the universities, I will give you mine for nothing.

BOOKWEIGHT
You shall have your money immediately; and pray remember, that I must have two Latin seditious mottoes and one Greek moral motto for pamphlets by to-morrow morning.

QUIBBLE
I want two Latin sentences, sir—one for page the fourth in the praise of loyalty, and another for page the tenth in praise of liberty and property.

DASH
The ghost would become a motto very well if you would bestow one on him.

BOOKWEIGHT
Let me have them all.

INDEX
Sir, I shall provide them. Be pleased to look on that, sir, and print me five hundred proposals and as many receipts.

BOOKWEIGHT
"Proposals for printing by subscription a New Translation of Cicero Of the Nature of the Gods, and his Tusculan Questions, by Jeremy Index, Esq." I am sorry you have undertaken this, for it prevents a design of mine.

INDEX
Indeed, sir, it does not; for you see all of the book that I ever intend to publish. It is only a handsome way of asking one's friends for a guinea.

BOOKWEIGHT
Then you have not translated a word of it, perhaps.

INDEX
Not a single syllable.

BOOKWEIGHT
Well, you shall have your proposals forthwith: but I desire you would be a little more reasonable in your bills for the future, or I shall deal with you no longer; for I have a certain fellow of a college, who offers to furnish me with second-hand mottoes out of the Spectator for twopence each.

INDEX
Sir, I only desire to live by my goods; and I hope you will be pleased to allow some difference between a neat fresh piece, piping hot out of the classicks, and old threadbare worn-out stuff that has past through every pedant's mouth and been as common at the universities as their whores.

BOOKWEIGHT, DASH, QUIBBLE, BLOTPAGE, SCARECROW.

SCARECROW
Sir, I have brought you a libel against the ministry.

BOOKWEIGHT [Aside]
Sir, I shall not take anything against them;—for I have two in the press already.

SCARECROW
Then, sir, I have an Apology in defence of them.

BOOKWEIGHT
That I shall not meddle with neither; they don't sell so well.

SCARECROW
I have a translation of Virgil's Aeneid, with notes on it, if we can agree about the price.

BOOKWEIGHT
Why, what price would you have?

SCARECROW
You shall read it first, otherwise how will you know the value?

BOOKWEIGHT
No, no, sir, I never deal that way—a poem is a poem, and a pamphlet a pamphlet with me. Give me a good handsome large volume, with a full promising title-page at the head of it, printed on a good paper and letter, the whole well bound and gilt, and I'll warrant its selling. You have the common error of authors, who think people buy books to read. No, no, books are only bought to furnish libraries, as pictures and glasses, and beds and chairs, are for other rooms. Look ye, sir, I don't like your title-page: however, to oblige a young beginner, I don't care if I do print it at my own expence.

SCARECROW
But pray, sir, at whose expence shall I eat?

BOOKWEIGHT
At whose? Why, at mine, sir, at mine. I am as great a friend to learning as the Dutch are to trade: no one can want bread with me who will earn it; therefore, sir, if you please to take your seat at my table, here will be everything necessary provided for you: good milk porridge, very often twice a day, which is good wholesome food and proper for students; a translator too is what I want at present, my last being in Newgate for shop-lifting. The rogue had a trick of translating out of the shops as well as the languages.

SCARECROW
But I am afraid I am not qualified for a translator, for I understand no language but my own.

BOOKWEIGHT
What, and translate Virgil?

SCARECROW
Alas! I translated him out of Dryden.

BOOKWEIGHT
Lay by your hat, sir—lay by your hat, and take your seat immediately. Not qualified!—thou art as well versed in thy trade as if thou hadst laboured in my garret these ten years. Let me tell you, friend, you will have more occasion for invention than learning here. You will be obliged to translate books out of all languages, especially French, that were never printed in any language whatsoever.

SCARECROW
Your trade abounds in mysteries.

BOOKWEIGHT
The study of bookselling is as difficult as the law: and there are as many tricks in the one as the other. Sometimes we give a foreign name to our own labours, and sometimes we put our names to the labours of others. Then, as the lawyers have John-a-Nokes and Tom-a-Stiles, so we have Messieurs Moore near St Paul's and Smith near the Royal Exchange.

SCENE VI

To them, **LUCKLESS**.

LUCKLESS
Mr Bookweight, your servant. Who can form to himself an idea more amiable than of a man at the head of so many patriots working for the benefit of their country.

BOOKWEIGHT
Truly, sir, I believe it is an idea more agreeable to you than that of a gentleman in the Crown-office paying thirty or forty guineas for abusing an honest tradesman.

LUCKLESS
Pshaw! that was only jocosely done, and a man who lives by wit must not be angry at a jest.

BOOKWEIGHT
Look ye, sir, if you have a mind to compromise the matter, and have brought me any money—

LUCKLESS
Hast thou been in thy trade so long, and talk of money to a modern author? You might as well have talked Latin or Greek to him. I have brought you paper, sir.

BOOKWEIGHT
That is not bringing me money, I own. Have you brought me an opera?

LUCKLESS
You may call it an opera if you will, but I call it a puppet-show.

BOOKWEIGHT
A puppet-show!

LUCKLESS
Ay, a puppet show; and is to be played this night at Drury-lane playhouse.

BOOKWEIGHT
A puppet-show in a playhouse!

LUCKLESS
Ay, why, what have been all the playhouses a long while but puppet-shows?

BOOKWEIGHT
Why, I don't know but it may succeed; at least if we can make out a tolerable good title-page: so, if you will walk in, if I can make a bargain with you I will. Gentlemen, you may go to dinner.

SCENE VII

Enter **JACK-PUDDING**, **DRUMMER**, **MOB**.

JACK-PUDDING
This is to give notice to all gentlemen, ladies, and others, that at the Theatre Royal in Drury-lane, this evening, will be performed the whole puppet-show called the Pleasures of the Town; in which will be shewn the whole court of nonsense, with abundance of singing, dancing, and several other entertainments: also the comical and diverting humours of Some-body and No-body; Punch and his wife Joan to be performed by figures, some of them six foot high. God save the King.

[Drum beats.

SCENE VIII

WITMORE with a paper, meeting **LUCKLESS**.

WITMORE
Oh! Luckless, I am overjoyed to meet you; here, take this paper, and you will be discouraged from writing, I warrant you.

LUCKLESS
What is it?—Oh! one of my play-bills.

WITMORE
One of thy play-bills!

LUCKLESS
Even so—I have taken the advice you gave me this morning.

WITMORE
Explain.

LUCKLESS
Why, I had some time since given this performance of mine to be rehearsed, and the actors were all perfect in their parts; but we happened to differ about some particulars, and I had a design to have given it over; 'till having my play refused by Marplay, I sent for the managers of the other house in a passion, joined issue with them, and this very evening it is to be acted.

WITMORE
Well, I wish you success.

LUCKLESS
Where are you going?

WITMORE
Anywhere but to hear you damned, which I must, was I to go to your puppet-show.

LUCKLESS
Indulge me in this trial; and I assure thee, if it be successless, it shall be the last.

WITMORE
On that condition I will; but should the torrent run against you, I shall be a fashionable friend and hiss with the rest.

LUCKLESS
No, a man who could do so unfashionable and so generous a thing as Mr Witmore did this morning——

WITMORE
Then I hope you will return it, by never mentioning it to me more. I will now to the pit.

LUCKLESS
And I behind the scenes.

SCENE IX

LUCKLESS, HARRIOT.

LUCKLESS
Dear Harriot!

HARRIOT

I was going to the playhouse to look after you—I am frightened out of my wits—I have left my mother at home with the strangest sort of man, who is inquiring after you: he has raised a mob before the door by the oddity of his appearance; his dress is like nothing I ever saw, and he talks of kings, and Bantam, and the strangest stuff.

LUCKLESS

What the devil can he be?

HARRIOT

One of your old acquaintance, I suppose, in disguise—one of his majesty's officers with his commission in his pocket, I warrant him.

LUCKLESS

Well, but have you your part perfect?

HARRIOT

I had, unless this fellow hath frightened it out of my head again; but I am afraid I shall play it wretchedly.

LUCKLESS

Why so?

HARRIOT

I shall never have assurance enough to go through with it, especially if they should hiss me.

LUCKLESS

Oh! your mask will keep you in countenance, and as for hissing, you need not fear it. The audience are generally so favourable to young beginners: but hist, here is your mother and she has seen us. Adieu, my dear, make what haste you can to the playhouse.

[Exit.

SCENE X

HARRIOT, MONEYWOOD.

HARRIOT

I wish I could avoid her, for I suppose we shall have an alarum.

MRS MONEYWOOD

So, so, very fine: always together, always caterwauling. How like a hangdog he stole off; and it's well for him he did, for I should have rung such a peal in his ears.—There's a friend of his at my house would be very glad of his company, and I wish it was in my power to bring them together.

HARRIOT

You would not surely be so barbarous.

MRS MONEYWOOD
Barbarous! ugh! You whining, puling fool! Hussey, you have not a drop of my blood in you. What, you are in love, I suppose?

HARRIOT
If I was, madam, it would be no crime,

MRS MONEYWOOD
Yes, madam, but it would, and a folly too. No woman of sense was ever in love with anything but a man's pocket. What, I suppose he has filled your head with a pack of romantick stuff of streams and dreams, and charms and arms. I know this is the stuff they all run on with, and so run into our debts, and run away with our daughters. Come, confess; are not you two to live in a wilderness together on love? Ah! thou fool! thou wilt find he will pay thee in love just as he has paid me in money. If thou wert resolved to go a-begging, why did you not follow the camp? There, indeed, you might have carried a knapsack; but here you will have no knapsack to carry. There, indeed, you might have had a chance of burying half a score husbands in a campaign; whereas a poet is a long-lived animal; you have but one chance of burying him, and that is, starving him.

HARRIOT
Well, madam, and I would sooner starve with the man I love than ride in a coach and six with him I hate: and, as for his passion, you will not make me suspect that, for he hath given me such proofs on't.

MRS MONEYWOOD
Proofs! I shall die. Has he given you proofs of love?

HARRIOT
All that any modest woman can require.

MRS MONEYWOOD
If he has given you all a modest woman can require, I am afraid he has given you more than a modest woman should take: because he has been so good a lodger, I suppose I shall have some more of the family to keep. It is probable I shall live to see half a dozen grandsons of mine in Grub-street.

SCENE XI

MONEYWOOD, HARRIOT, JACK.

JACK
Oh, madam! the man whom you took for a bailiff is certainly some great man; he has a vast many jewels and other fine things about him; he offered me twenty guineas to shew him my master, and has given away so much money among the chairmen, that some folks believe he intends to stand member of parliament for Westminster.

MRS MONEYWOOD

Nay, then, I am sure he is worth inquiring into. So, d'ye hear, sirrah, make as much haste as you can before me, and desire him to part with no more money till I come.

HARRIOT
So, now my mother is in pursuit of money, I may securely go in pursuit of my lover: and I am mistaken, good mamma, if e'en you would not think that the better pursuit of the two.
In generous love transporting raptures lie,
Which age, with all its treasures, cannot buy.

Henry Fielding – A Short Biography

Henry Fielding was born at Sharpham Park, near Glastonbury, in Somerset on April 22nd 1707. His early years were spent on his parents' farm in Dorset. His family were well to do. His father was a colonel, later a general in the army, his maternal grandfather was a judge of the Queen's Bench and his second cousin would later become the fourth Earl of Denbigh.

He was educated at Eton where he became lifelong friends with William Pitt the Elder.

An early romance ended disastrously and with it his removal to London and the beginnings of a glittering literary career. Early advice on this came from another cousin, the noted poet, Lady Mary Wortley Montagu. Fielding published his first play, at age 21, in 1728.

Later that same year he journeyed to the University at Leiden, the oldest University in Holland, to study classics and law. However, within months, with funds low, mainly due to his father cutting off his allowance, he was forced to return to London and to write for the theatre.

It was a twist of fate that was to ensure him both notoriety and a reputation that would exceed his wildest expectations.

He was prolific, sometimes writing six plays a year, but he did like to poke fun at the authorities. His plays were thought to be the final straw for the authorities in their attempts to bring some sense of order to an increasingly provocative Theatre. Some of the plays denigrated, insulted, or criticised either the King, or his Government, in ways that caused them to react with their preferred response; a new law. Although the Golden Rump was cited as the play on which the authorities based their need for better regulation it is thought that the constant stepping over the line by Fielding in his own works was the actual trigger for, and target of, the new law. No copy of the play, The Golden Rump, exists today and it seems never, in fact, to have been performed or perhaps even published. Various accounts attribute Fielding as the author and others say it was secretly commissioned by Walpole himself to bring about the conditions necessary to bring the Act before Parliament.

Whatever the validity in 1737 The Theatrical Licensing Act was passed. At a stroke political satire was almost impossible. Fielding much admired – and reviled – for his savaging of Sir Robert Walpole government was rendered mute. Any playwright who was viewed with suspicion by the Government now found an audience difficult to find and therefore Theatre owners now toed the Government line, works only being available for performance after review by the Lord Chamberlain. A process that was to last in England, although greatly amended in 1843, until 1968.

Fielding was practical in the circumstances and ironically stopped writing to once again take up his career in the practice of law. He became a barrister after studying at Middle Temple – he completed the six year course in only three. By this time he had also married Charlotte Craddock, his first wife, and they would go on to have five children, but only a daughter would survive. Charlotte died in 1744 but was immortalised as the heroine in both Tom Jones and Amelia.

As a businessman Fielding lacked any financial education and he and his family often endured bouts of poverty. He did however find a wealthy benefactor in the shape of Ralph Allen, who was to later feature in the novel Tom Jones as the character foundation for Squire Allworthy.

Fielding never stopped writing political satire or satires of current arts and letters. The Tragedy of Tragedies, for which Hogarth designed the frontispiece, had, for example, some success as a printed play. He also contributed a number of works to journals of the day as well as writing for Tory periodicals, usually under the name of "Captain Hercules Vinegar". His choice of name reveals his style. But then again his other later nom de plumes are also revealing; Sir Alexander Drawcansir and Scriblerus Secundus

In 1731 Fielding wrote "The Roast Beef of Old England", which is used by the Royal Navy and the United States Marine Corps. It was later arranged by Richard Leveridge.

During the late 1730s and early 1740s Fielding continued to air his liberal and anti-Jacobite views in satirical articles and newspapers. He was nothing if not passionate and this adherence to principles would eventually have great reward for him.

Fielding was much put out by the success of Samuel Richardson's Pamela, or Virtue Rewarded. His reaction was to spur him into writing a novel. In 1741 this first novel, Shamela, was a success, an anonymous parody of Richardson's melodramatic novel. It is a satire that follows the model of the famous Tory satirists of the previous generation; Swift and Gay.

On the tail of this success came Joseph Andrews in 1742. Begun as a parody on Pamela's brother, Joseph, it swiftly developed and matured into an accomplished novel in its own right and marked the entrance of Fielding as a major English novelist.

In 1743, he published a novel in the Miscellanies volume III (which was, in fact, the first volume of the Miscellanies). This was The History of the Life of the Late Mr Jonathan Wild the Great. Sometimes this is cited as his first novel, as he did indeed begin writing it before Shamela, but it is now placed later. Once again Fielding returns to satire and one of his favourite subjects – Sir Robert Walpole. In it he draws a parallel between Walpole and Jonathan Wild, the infamous gang leader and highwayman. He implicitly compares the Whig party in Parliament to a gang of thieves, whose leader, Walpole, lives only for his desire and ambition to be a "Great Man" (a common epithet for Walpole) and should culminate only in the antithesis of greatness: being hung from a gallows. By now Walpole had resigned as Prime minster after some 20 years. Fielding could now re-affirm political allegiance back to the Whigs and would now denounce both Tories and Jacobites in his writings.

Although Fielding was never afraid to court controversy he published his next work anonymously in 1746, and perhaps with good reason. The Female Husband, a fictionalized account of a sensational case of a female transvestite who was tried for duping another woman into marriage. This was one of a number of small published pamphlets at sixpence a time. Though a minor item in both length and his canon it shows Fielding's consistent interest and examination of fraud, sham, and masks but, of course, his subject matter was rather sensational.

In 1747, three years after Charlotte's death and ignoring public opinion, he married her former maid, Mary Daniel, who was pregnant. Mary bore him five children altogether; three daughters, who died early and sons William and Allen.

Undoubtedly the masterpiece of Fielding's career was the novel Tom Jones, published in 1749. It is a wonderfully and carefully constructed picaresque novel following the convoluted and hilarious tale of how a foundling came into a fortune.

Fielding was a consistent anti-Jacobite and a keen supporter of the Church of England. This led to him now being richly rewarded with the position of London's Chief Magistrate. The position itself had no salary attached but he refused all manner of bribes during his tenure, which was most unusual. Fielding continued to write and his career both literary and professional continued to climb.

In 1749 he joined with his younger half-brother John, to help found what was the nascent forerunner to a London police force, the Bow Street Runners. (He and his siblings were quite some partnership. His younger sister, Sarah, also became a well known novelist)

His influence here was undoubted. He and John did much to help the cause of judicial reform and to help improve prison conditions. His pamphlets and enquiries included a proposal for the abolition of public hangings. This was not, as you would think because he was opposed to capital punishment as such—indeed, for example, in his 1751 presiding over the trial of the notorious criminal James Field, he found him guilty in a robbery and sentenced him to hang.

In January 1752 Fielding started a fortnightly periodical titled The Covent-Garden Journal, which he would publish under the colourful pseudonym of "Sir Alexander Drawcansir, Knt. Censor of Great Britain" until November of the same year. In this periodical, Fielding directly challenged the "armies of Grub Street" and the other periodical writers of the day in a conflict that would eventually become the Paper War of 1752–3.

Fielding then published, in 1753, "Examples of the interposition of Providence in the Detection and Punishment of Murder, a work in which, rejecting the deistic and materialistic visions of the world, he wrote in favour of the belief in God's presence and divine judgement, arguing that the rise of murder rates was due to neglect of the Christian religion. In 1753 he would add to this with Proposals for making an effectual Provision for the Poor.

Fielding's ardent commitment to the cause of justice as a great humanitarian in the 1750s unfortunately coincided with a rapid deterioration in his health. Such was his decline that in the summer of 1754 he travelled, with Mary and his daughter, to Portugal in search of a cure. Gout, asthma, dropsy and other afflictions forced him to use crutches. His health continued to fail alarmingly.

Henry Fielding died in Lisbon two months later on October 8th, 1754.

His tomb is in the city's English Cemetery (Cemitério Inglês), which is now the graveyard of St. George's Church, Lisbon.

Henry Fielding – A Concise Bibliography

The Masquerade, a poem
Love in Several Masques, a play, 1728
Rape Upon Rape, a play, 1730.
The Temple Beau, a play, 1730
The Author's Farce, a play, 1730
The Letter Writers, a play, 1731
The Tragedy of Tragedies; or, The Life and Death of Tom Thumb the Great, a play, 1731
Grub-Street Opera, a play, 1731
The Roast Beef of Old England, 1731
The Modern Husband, a play, 1732
The Mock Doctor, a play, 1732
The Lottery, a play, 1732
The Covent Garden Tragedy, a play, 1732
The Miser, a play, 1732
The Old Debauchees, a play 1732
The Intriguing Chambermaid, a play, 1734
Don Quixote in England, a play, 1734
Pasquin, a play, 1736
Eurydice Hiss'd, a play, 1737
The Historical Register for the Year 1736, a play, 1737
An Apology for the Life of Mrs. Shamela Andrews, a novel, 1741
The History of the Adventures of Joseph Andrews & his Friend, Mr. Abraham Abrams, a novel, 1742
The Life and Death of Jonathan Wild, the Great, a novel, 1743.
Miscellanies – collection of works, 1743, contained the poem Part of Juvenal's Sixth Satire, Modernized in Burlesque Verse
The Female Husband or the Surprising History of Mrs Mary alias Mr George Hamilton, who was convicted of having married a young woman of Wells and lived with her as her husband, taken from her own mouth since her confinement, a pamphlet, fictionalized report, 1746
The History of Tom Jones, a Foundling, a novel, 1749
A Journey from this World to the Next – 1749
Amelia, a novel, 1751
"Examples of the interposition of Providence in the Detection and Punishment of Murder containing above thirty cases in which this dreadful crime has been brought to light in the most extraordinary and miraculous manner; collected from various authors, ancient and modern", 1752
The Covent Garden Journal, a periodical, 1752
Journal of a Voyage to Lisbon, a travel narrative, 1755
The Fathers: Or, the Good-Natur'd Man, a play, published posthumously in 1778

Other Works (Undated)
An Old Man or The Virgin Unmasked
Miss Lucy in Town, a Play, a sequel to The Virgin Unmasked
Plutus with William Young from the Greek play by Aristophanes.

The Temple Beau, a play
The Wedding Beau, a play
The Welsh Opera
Tumble-Down Dick
An Essay on Conversation, an Essay
The True Patriot, a letter

Printed in Great Britain
by Amazon

52352335R00024